TIMES TABLES 1 to 20

HERMES
HOUSE

1 TIMES TABLE

0	×	1	=	0
1	×	1	=	1
2	×	1	=	2
3	×	1	=	3
4	×	1	=	4
5	×	1	=	5
6	×	1	=	6
7	×	1	=	7
8	×	1	=	8
9	×	1	=	9
10	×	1	=	10
11	×	1	=	11
12	×	1	=	12

2 TIMES TABLE

$0 \times 2 = 0$

$1 \times 2 = 2$

$2 \times 2 = 4$

$3 \times 2 = 6$

$4 \times 2 = 8$

$5 \times 2 = 10$

$6 \times 2 = 12$

$7 \times 2 = 14$

$8 \times 2 = 16$

$9 \times 2 = 18$

$10 \times 2 = 20$

$11 \times 2 = 22$

$12 \times 2 = 24$

3 TIMES TABLE

$0 \times 3 = 0$

$1 \times 3 = 3$

$2 \times 3 = 6$

$3 \times 3 = 9$

$4 \times 3 = 12$

$5 \times 3 = 15$

$6 \times 3 = 18$

$7 \times 3 = 21$

$8 \times 3 = 24$

$9 \times 3 = 27$

$10 \times 3 = 30$

$11 \times 3 = 33$

$12 \times 3 = 36$

4 TIMES TABLE

0	×	4	=	0
1	×	4	=	4
2	×	4	=	8
3	×	4	=	12
4	×	4	=	16
5	×	4	=	20
6	×	4	=	24
7	×	4	=	28
8	×	4	=	32
9	×	4	=	36
10	×	4	=	40
11	×	4	=	44
12	×	4	=	48

5 TIMES TABLE

$$0 \times 5 = 0$$
$$1 \times 5 = 5$$
$$2 \times 5 = 10$$
$$3 \times 5 = 15$$
$$4 \times 5 = 20$$
$$5 \times 5 = 25$$
$$6 \times 5 = 30$$
$$7 \times 5 = 35$$
$$8 \times 5 = 40$$
$$9 \times 5 = 45$$
$$10 \times 5 = 50$$
$$11 \times 5 = 55$$
$$12 \times 5 = 60$$

6 TIMES TABLE

$0 \times 6 = 0$

$1 \times 6 = 6$

$2 \times 6 = 12$

$3 \times 6 = 18$

$4 \times 6 = 24$

$5 \times 6 = 30$

$6 \times 6 = 36$

$7 \times 6 = 42$

$8 \times 6 = 48$

$9 \times 6 = 54$

$10 \times 6 = 60$

$11 \times 6 = 66$

$12 \times 6 = 72$

7 TIMES TABLE

$0 \times 7 = 0$

$1 \times 7 = 7$

$2 \times 7 = 14$

$3 \times 7 = 21$

$4 \times 7 = 28$

$5 \times 7 = 35$

$6 \times 7 = 42$

$7 \times 7 = 49$

$8 \times 7 = 56$

$9 \times 7 = 63$

$10 \times 7 = 70$

$11 \times 7 = 77$

$12 \times 7 = 84$

$0 \times 8 = 0$

$1 \times 8 = 8$

$2 \times 8 = 16$

$3 \times 8 = 24$

$4 \times 8 = 32$

$5 \times 8 = 40$

$6 \times 8 = 48$

$7 \times 8 = 56$

$8 \times 8 = 64$

$9 \times 8 = 72$

$10 \times 8 = 80$

$11 \times 8 = 88$

$12 \times 8 = 96$

9 TIMES TABLE

$$0 \times 9 = 0$$
$$1 \times 9 = 9$$
$$2 \times 9 = 18$$
$$3 \times 9 = 27$$
$$4 \times 9 = 36$$
$$5 \times 9 = 45$$
$$6 \times 9 = 54$$
$$7 \times 9 = 63$$
$$8 \times 9 = 72$$
$$9 \times 9 = 81$$
$$10 \times 9 = 90$$
$$11 \times 9 = 99$$
$$12 \times 9 = 108$$

10 TIMES TABLE

$$0 \times 10 = 0$$
$$1 \times 10 = 10$$
$$2 \times 10 = 20$$
$$3 \times 10 = 30$$
$$4 \times 10 = 40$$
$$5 \times 10 = 50$$
$$6 \times 10 = 60$$
$$7 \times 10 = 70$$
$$8 \times 10 = 80$$
$$9 \times 10 = 90$$
$$10 \times 10 = 100$$
$$11 \times 10 = 110$$
$$12 \times 10 = 120$$

0	×	11	=	0
1	×	11	=	11
2	×	11	=	22
3	×	11	=	33
4	×	11	=	44
5	×	11	=	55
6	×	11	=	66
7	×	11	=	77
8	×	11	=	88
9	×	11	=	99
10	×	11	=	110
11	×	11	=	121
12	×	11	=	132

12 TIMES TABLE

$0 \times 12 = 0$

$1 \times 12 = 12$

$2 \times 12 = 24$

$3 \times 12 = 36$

$4 \times 12 = 48$

$5 \times 12 = 60$

$6 \times 12 = 72$

$7 \times 12 = 84$

$8 \times 12 = 96$

$9 \times 12 = 108$

$10 \times 12 = 120$

$11 \times 12 = 132$

$12 \times 12 = 144$

13 TIMES TABLE

0	×	13	=	0
1	×	13	=	13
2	×	13	=	26
3	×	13	=	39
4	×	13	=	52
5	×	13	=	65
6	×	13	=	78
7	×	13	=	91
8	×	13	=	104
9	×	13	=	117
10	×	13	=	130
11	×	13	=	143
12	×	13	=	156

14 TIMES TABLE

$$0 \times 14 = 0$$
$$1 \times 14 = 14$$
$$2 \times 14 = 28$$
$$3 \times 14 = 42$$
$$4 \times 14 = 56$$
$$5 \times 14 = 70$$
$$6 \times 14 = 84$$
$$7 \times 14 = 98$$
$$8 \times 14 = 112$$
$$9 \times 14 = 126$$
$$10 \times 14 = 140$$
$$11 \times 14 = 154$$
$$12 \times 14 = 168$$

15 TIMES TABLE

0	×	15	=	0
1	×	15	=	15
2	×	15	=	30
3	×	15	=	45
4	×	15	=	60
5	×	15	=	75
6	×	15	=	90
7	×	15	=	105
8	×	15	=	120
9	×	15	=	135
10	×	15	=	150
11	×	15	=	165
12	×	15	=	180

16 TIMES TABLE

$$0 \times 16 = 0$$
$$1 \times 16 = 16$$
$$2 \times 16 = 32$$
$$3 \times 16 = 48$$
$$4 \times 16 = 64$$
$$5 \times 16 = 80$$
$$6 \times 16 = 96$$
$$7 \times 16 = 112$$
$$8 \times 16 = 128$$
$$9 \times 16 = 144$$
$$10 \times 16 = 160$$
$$11 \times 16 = 176$$
$$12 \times 16 = 192$$

17 TIMES TABLE

0	×	17	=	0
1	×	17	=	17
2	×	17	=	34
3	×	17	=	51
4	×	17	=	68
5	×	17	=	85
6	×	17	=	102
7	×	17	=	119
8	×	17	=	136
9	×	17	=	153
10	×	17	=	170
11	×	17	=	187
12	×	17	=	204

18 TIMES TABLE

0	×	18	=	0
1	×	18	=	18
2	×	18	=	36
3	×	18	=	54
4	×	18	=	72
5	×	18	=	90
6	×	18	=	108
7	×	18	=	126
8	×	18	=	144
9	×	18	=	162
10	×	18	=	180
11	×	18	=	198
12	×	18	=	216

19 TIMES TABLE

0	×	19	=	0
1	×	19	=	19
2	×	19	=	38
3	×	19	=	57
4	×	19	=	76
5	×	19	=	95
6	×	19	=	114
7	×	19	=	133
8	×	19	=	152
9	×	19	=	171
10	×	19	=	190
11	×	19	=	209
12	×	19	=	228

20 TIMES TABLE

$0 \times 20 = 0$

$1 \times 20 = 20$

$2 \times 20 = 40$

$3 \times 20 = 60$

$4 \times 20 = 80$

$5 \times 20 = 100$

$6 \times 20 = 120$

$7 \times 20 = 140$

$8 \times 20 = 160$

$9 \times 20 = 180$

$10 \times 20 = 200$

$11 \times 20 = 220$

$12 \times 20 = 240$

	1	2	3	4	5	6	7	8	9	10
0	0	0	0	0	0	0	0	0	0	0
1	1	2	3	4	5	6	7	8	9	10
2	2	4	6	8	10	12	14	16	18	20
3	3	6	9	12	15	18	21	24	27	30
4	4	8	12	16	20	24	28	32	36	40
5	5	10	15	20	25	30	35	40	45	50
6	6	12	18	24	30	36	42	48	54	60
7	7	14	21	28	35	42	49	56	63	70
8	8	16	24	32	40	48	56	64	72	80
9	9	18	27	36	45	54	63	72	81	90
10	10	20	30	40	50	60	70	80	90	100
11	11	22	33	44	55	66	77	88	99	110
12	12	24	36	48	60	72	84	96	108	120

NUMBER MATRIX

11	12	13	14	15	16	17	18	19	20
0	0	0	0	0	0	0	0	0	0
11	12	13	14	15	16	17	18	19	20
22	24	26	28	30	32	34	36	38	40
33	36	39	42	45	48	51	54	57	60
44	48	52	56	60	64	68	72	76	80
55	60	65	70	75	80	85	90	95	100
66	72	78	84	90	96	102	108	114	120
77	84	91	98	105	112	119	126	133	140
88	96	104	112	120	128	136	144	152	160
99	108	117	126	135	144	153	162	171	180
110	120	130	140	150	160	170	180	190	200
121	132	143	154	165	176	187	198	209	220
132	144	156	168	180	192	204	216	228	240

This edition is published by Hermes House,
an imprint of Anness Publishing Ltd,
Blaby Road, Wigston, Leicestershire LE18 4SE

Email: info@anness.com

Web: www.hermeshouse.com; www.annesspublishing.com

If you like the images in this book and would like to investigate using
them for publishing, promotions or advertising, please visit
our website www.practicalpictures.com for more information.

ETHICAL TRADING POLICY
At Anness Publishing we believe that business should be conducted in an ethical
and ecologically sustainable way, with respect for the environment and a proper
regard to the replacement of the natural resources we employ.
As a publisher, we use a lot of wood pulp in high-quality paper for printing, and
that wood commonly comes from spruce trees. We are therefore currently
growing more than 750,000 trees in three Scottish forest plantations: Berrymoss
(130 hectares/320 acres), West Touxhill (125 hectares/305 acres) and Deveron
Forest (75 hectares/185 acres).
The forests we manage contain more than 3.5 times the number of trees employed
each year in making paper for the books we manufacture.
Because of this ongoing ecological investment programme, you, as our customer,
can have the pleasure and reassurance of knowing that a tree is being cultivated on
your behalf to naturally replace the materials used to make the book you are holding.
Our forestry programme is run in accordance with the UK Woodland Assurance
Scheme (UKWAS) and will be certified by the internationally recognized Forest
Stewardship Council (FSC). The FSC is a non-government organization dedicated
to promoting responsible management of the world's forests. Certification ensures
forests are managed in an environmentally sustainable and socially responsible way.
For further information about this scheme, go to www.annesspublishing.com/trees

A CIP catalogue record for this book is available from the British Library.

PUBLISHER'S NOTE
Although the advice and information in this book are believed to be accurate and true
at the time of going to press, neither the authors nor the publisher can accept any
legal responsibility or liability for any errors or omissions that may have been made.

Manufacturer: Anness Publishing Ltd, Blaby Road,
Wigston, Leicestershire LE18 4SE, England
For Product Tracking go to: www.annesspublishing.com/tracking
Batch: 5495-21289-0004